Abigail Ene Fatoki

MORE THAN *gods*

More Than Gods

ISBN: 978-978-60982-2-7

Published and printed by:

Pen-Impact Writing and Publishing Enterprise
16 Adedoyin Rhodes-Vivour Close, Asokoro,
Abuja, FCT, Nigeria
Website: www.pen-impact.com
Email: info@pen-impact.com
Tel: +234 701 990 4999

NATIONAL LIBRARY OF NIGERIA CATALOGUING-IN-PUBLICATION DATA
More Than Gods
FATOKI, Abigail Ene
1. Christian life
2. Revivals
I. Title

BV4501.3.F254 2024 248.4
ISBN: 978-978-60982-2-7 (pbk) AACR2

CONTENTS

INTRODUCTION

THE BEGINNING OF SUFFERING

If you look around our society, you will see so much suffering and pain. Irrespective of the innumerable number of philanthropic individuals and organisations in our world, who labour to reduce the suffering of people, yet suffering persists. It seems as though life itself is full of episodic cycles of suffering for different people at different times. It is common to hear people whine as they wonder, "why did God create man to suffer, when He has what it takes to remove suffering from our lives?".

Could it be that God has a reason for which He allowed suffering to be an inevitable part of our earthly sojourn? I have personally pondered on this question on a number of occasions.

One day, as I was taking a shower and thinking of what I had watched on the news earlier, all I could see was the devastation, hunger, poverty, hate, and evil of every kind that existed on both the earth and the hearts and minds of people. I was angry in my spirit, and I jokingly asked the Holy Spirit, why then were humans (man) created? Is it that we were created to suffer? If so, what is the essence of life and living? Why did God even create us?

Then, right there, overshadowing the sound of running water, the Holy Spirit ministered to me saying: "God created man for His pleasure."

REVELATION 4:11

"Thou art worthy, O Lord, to receive glory and honour and power: for thou, hast created all things, and for thy pleasure, they are and were created."

He went on to open my eyes to the fact that man was created to praise God, honor God, glorify God, fellowship with God, and reference His majestic power.

The ability to create man for His pleasure, and cause Him to replicate and multiply, is one of the numerous things, many of which we will consider in this book, that sets God apart from other gods. God has the power to bring whatever He desires into creation, and all that He creates is good; beautifully made with splendour and greatness that can't be explained by mere human knowledge. We also, as His creation, have the ability to replicate ourselves by giving birth to our children.

The Spirit of the Lord then continued to say to me: God did not intend for man to suffer. The spirit of the Most High God said to me: "Can't you see everything that was made beautiful are all in their perfect features and placement?"

The Holy Spirit continued to minister to me, saying that God created everything that would make man comfortable on earth. The Almighty made light, the waters, the heavens, dry land, the firmament, evening, morning, day and night, seas, grass, trees, herbs, fruits, seasons (winter- raining season, summer- dry season, and autumn), years and days, stars, living creatures in the waters, and birds that fly above the earth. The Almighty made the great waters, as well as all living creatures according to their kind, cattle of all kinds, creeping things of all kinds, beasts of all kinds, such as the moon, mountains, etc. (Genesis 1:1-31).

In the creation of man, God made man in His image and likeness, making us a photocopy of Himself. He created man to be like a god on earth. This is why Psalm 82:6 explains: *"Ye are gods, and all of you are the children of the most high".*

However, man in his error and poor understanding of whom God had created him to be, went on to create other gods out of their own hands and their own imaginations. By doing these, they gave room to demons to operate in the guise of gods. The demons became gods to many. This is why the Bible in Deuteronomy 32:16-17 says:

> *"They stirred him to jealousy with strange gods, with abominations they provoked him to anger. They sacrificed to demons that were no gods, to gods they had never known".*

A very important fact to know is that there is no other God, there can never be another. So these gods are truly not in the nature of God. In Isaiah 43:10, the Lord God said *"You are My witnesses," says the LORD, "And My servant whom I have chosen, That you may know and believe Me, And understand that I am He. Before Me there was no God formed, Nor shall there be after Me"*

If there is any manifestation that arises from interactions with these gods or in the worship of these gods, they are simply orchestrated by the evil spirits (demons/fallen angels) who have taken hold of this idolatry of mankind to operate.

This is why Apostle Paul further explained these gods in 1 Corinthians 10:20-22, as he addressed the church in Corinthia, he said "What do I imply then? That food offered to idols is anything, or that an idol is anything? No, I imply that what pagans sacrifice they offer to demons and not to God. I do not want you to be participants with demons. You cannot drink the cup of the Lord and the cup of demons. You cannot partake of the table of the Lord and the table of demons. Shall we provoke the Lord to jealousy? Are we stronger than Him?"

This deviation of the heart of man from God, is where the human suffering started. As they gave themselves to the worship of these gods that are products of their minds and hands, these demons began to influence the actions of man, causing mankind to live in the way God did not intend for them to live. From the time of Adam and Eve, this had been this case; the moment Eve and Adam sinned.

Sadly, in this day and time, the worship of other gods is on the increase, even new gods are being brought forth. Many who before now called on the name of the Lord, are beginning to submit themselves to these gods. Many others try to play the two sides, they are with God Almighty on Sundays, and after that day, they go to the streams, the oceans, the shrines, the bushes to also meddle in the worship of other gods.

This is why in this book, I will be casting light on the one true God as the Almighty God among other gods. This book will also expose the evil works of these gods and their impact in the life of mankind. This book has one goal, to stir your heart into true worship of the Almighty God, and to shun any form of meddling with any other god.

CHAPTER ONE

THE NATURE OF GOD

One of the things that sets God Almighty apart from all other gods is His nature. Apart from His nature as God Almighty - the uncreated creator, in this chapter we are going to be discussing other attributes of God that makes Him incomparable to any other god.

- **His loving nature**

The Almighty God is a loving God. Among all other gods, none of them can measure up in the place of love, none can love you enough to die for you. However, God Almighty loves us a lot. He not only made us in His image and likeness, He did not only die for us to redeem us, but He went ahead to make a dwelling place in us.

1 JOHN 4:16

"And we have known and believed the love that God hath to us. God is love, and he that dwelt in love dwelt in God and God in him."

We can see that in His creation, He made love and marriage between a man and a woman; we humans also love our children unconditionally. Those are the attributes and nature of our Creator, LOVE! That is in us also.

- **The Kindness Attribute**

The Almighty God is kind. Among these other gods, none of them stood out in kindness enough to even compare. Isaiah 54:8 says: *"In a surge of anger I hid my face from you for a moment, but with everlasting kindness, I will have compassion on you," says the Lord your Redeemer."*

He is the Most merciful, the Most Holy and Just Lord (1 Samuel 2:2, Deuteronomy 32:4, Exodus 34:6-7), God Almighty is the most powerful among the gods (Isaiah 41:10).

The Spirit of the Lord then said to me: Humans suffer today because the gods got jealous of God's creation, especially man, whom He made in His image and likeness, and man should live like their Creator, living holy and pure like the Almighty God. The jealous gods don't have the power, ability, and even dominion to make replicas of themselves to worship them. They then went into the hearts of men to corrupt it (Genesis Chapter 3) from the nature of God from which man was made.

The Spirit of the Lord then said to me: The jealous gods know and understand God's nature of holiness and purity and that He can't get close to anything that is impure and corrupt, evil, hateful, unkind, unloving, unjust, lies, jealousy, wickedness, pride, boastful, lustful, and all sort of evil and corruption that is present with man in these last days (Habakkuk 1:13, 12:14). The gods pollute God's creation and separate man from God, who is our Father, our Maker, our love, our Creator and our God. These gods are trickery and mostly sly in nature. They don't possess the ultimate power but operate in deception, fraud, manipulation, counterfeiting and faking. They destroyed the relationship God has with us humans.

After the last word by the Holy Spirit, I was out of the shower, praising God and singing thou art worthy, oh Lord, to receive glory, honour and power for thou had created all things and for thy pleasure, they were all well created (Revelation 11:4).

Praise the Lord!

CHAPTER TWO

WHY MEN DIE

Many of us get weary of going through the hardship of life only to die. Almost every time there is the news of an untimely death, you would hear many ask the question - "What then is the purpose of this life? Why do we have to go through all the suffering that life is filled with, only to die?"

I have been in such a situation myself, where I had similar questions. I woke up on the 27th day of January in the year 2024; that was after the day I asked the Holy Spirit why men who are God's creation are suffering with so much pain and all sorts of agony on earth. It was there that the Holy Spirit ministered all those words to me in chapter one of this book.

I was still lying down on my bed when I asked the Holy Spirit those questions. Over the years, I have built a relationship with the Holy Spirit, and the Holy Spirit of God revealed Himself to me in a dream in the year 2010. It was a time I was in so much distress; the Spirit of God revealed himself to me and told me that He was the Spirit of Light and the Spirit of Truth. Before that dream, I never knew the Holy Spirit was referred to as the Spirit of Light and the Spirit of Truth until I heard Bishop David Oyedepo, the founder of Winners Chapel Worldwide, during a Shiloh programme for that year. The Bishop sighted a verse from the Bible in the book of John 16:13-14. Right there, I went to that verse of the Bible, and I read it over and over again.

"But when he, the Spirit of truth, comes, he will guide you into all the truth. He will not speak on his own; he will speak only what he hears, and he will tell you what is yet to come. He will glorify me because it is from me that he will receive what he will make known to you."

That was when I started my relationship with the Holy Spirit. I speak to Him like a brother, a friend, a teacher, a helper and most importantly, my comforter, the enabler, the wisdom of the Highest God, my strength, the Spirit of Fire, and my guide. I speak to Him, and most of the time, He answers me. But there are also times He says nothing.

Let me go back to what I asked the Holy Spirit while I was still lying on my bed that day. That day, I wondered why God made us for His pleasure and why it became possible for other gods to seize the hearts of men to corrupt the nature of God in us and then, in turn, destroy the relationship of God with us.

Why do men die? Why do men give birth, live and then die? Why? Can't God stop men from procreating so that they don't have to suffer the sorrow of death anymore and probably put an end to man and human suffering?

GENESIS 2:17

"But you must not eat from the tree of the knowledge of good and evil, for when you eat from it you will certainly die"

Man must die because the nature we carry now has been corrupted. This is not the nature that God created man to be in when he planned eternity for man. Therefore, man must die so that this nature and even these physical forms can return to the state God had in mind at creation, the state that can live forever without sin and disobedience.

Just imagine for a second if men were to live forever with this corrupted nature. They would destroy all of God's creation on earth and turn themselves into gods. Having been made in the image of God, men possess the ability of the Creator. That is why today, you see men exploring space, going to the moon, and inventing all sorts of technology and its advancement. They make planes and drones that fly in the sky like birds; they explore other planets apart from the earth, where God kept them. With the present advanced technology in AI, humans can do the unimaginable. All of these are expressions of God Almighty's creative abilities that were deposited in man.

If men don't grow old and die in this conceited nature, with all the abilities they have, they will turn themselves into gods and consider themselves invincible. They will also continue to yield to these other gods, who lure and manipulate the hearts of men.

The Holy Spirit then said to me that man possesses the power and the nature of the Most High but in corrupted form and has to die.

CHAPTER 3

THE CREATIVE POWER OF GOD

In this chapter, we will be looking at the creative power of God that is expressed in man. As I lightly discussed in chapter two, one of the things that set our God apart from any other deity worshiped by man is the fact that God Almighty can create. He is a creative God, and this creative power has also been deposited in man.

It is this same nature that is in man: causing him to desire for success, achievement. and striving towards perfection. It is His light in us humans that drives us each day to strive to be winners in all that we do.

This explains why humans create. We create because we are made in the image of God. Genesis 1:27 states, *"So God created mankind in His own image, in the image of God He created them; male and female He created them."* This divine likeness includes the ability to create, innovate, and bring new things into existence, reflecting God's own creative nature.

God, knowing what He deposited inside of us, granted us dominion over the earth and its creatures, as seen in Genesis 1:28:

"God blessed them and said to them, 'Be fruitful and increase in number; fill the earth and subdue it. Rule over the fish in the sea and the birds in the sky and over every living creature that moves on the ground."

This dominion is not just about control but also about stewardship. Humans are responsible for managing and caring for God's creation wisely and sustainably, reflecting the divine governance in our earthly responsibilities.

EXPRESSIONS OF THE CREATIVE POWER OF GOD

IN ESTABLISHING HIS DOMINION on earth, man partners with God by expressing His creative power and carrying out certain responsibilities in the maintenance of God's creations and continuation of God's creativity. The avenues through which man do this include the following:

Procreation

One of the most profound ways humans reflect God's creative power is through birthing and procreation. The ability to bring new life into the world is a direct reflection of God's creative act. It showcases the continuation of life and the perpetuation of human existence, symbolising the ongoing creative work of God.

GENESIS 1:28

"And God bless them, and God said unto them, be fruitful, and multiply, and replenish the earth, and subdue it; and have dominion over the fish of the sea, and over the fowl of the air, and over every living thing that moves upon the earth."

The Spirit of the Most High ministered this word to me: Man must continue to procreate because that is the commandment of God.

Artistic Expressions

This creative power is also found in the artistic expressions of man. In Exodus 31:1–5, God specifically anoints Bezalel with skills for artistic craftsmanship:

> *"Then the Lord said to Moses, 'See, I have chosen Bezalel, son of Uri, the son of Hur, of the tribe of Judah, and I have filled him with the Spirit of God, with wisdom, with understanding, with knowledge and with all kinds of skills—to make artistic designs for work in gold, silver, and bronze, to cut and set stones, to work in wood, and to engage in all kinds of crafts."*

These talents contribute to the rich tapestry of human culture, allowing us to express creativity in various forms, such as art, music, literature, and technology.

Social Interaction

Human creativity is also fueled by social interaction. In Genesis 2:18, God says, *"It is not good for the man to be alone. I will make a helper suitable for him."* This indicates that human relationships and community are essential for fostering creativity. Collaboration and the sharing of ideas enhance our ability to create and innovate.

Advancements in Technology and Medical Science

God has endowed humans with the knowledge and understanding to advance in technology and medical science. These advancements are seen as extensions of God's creative power, enabling humans to improve their quality of life, solve complex problems, and heal diseases.

EZEKIEL 47:12

"Fruit trees of all kinds will grow on both banks of the river. Their leaves will not wither, nor will their fruit fail. Every month, they will

bear fruit because the water from the sanctuary flows to them. Their fruit will serve for food, and their leaves for healing."

Innovations in these fields reflect the wisdom and intellect bestowed upon humanity by God, showcasing our ability to harness and develop the natural world for the betterment of society.

The Spirit of the Lord ministered these very words to me in one of the early hours of the day, and the Holy Spirit said to me again:

"Also, do you know why humans can explore the moon and other planets above the earth? Even though men don't have dominion there?"

I asked why, and the Spirit of the Lord then said to me that it's because God the Almighty wants His creation to see His splendor and glory and believe in His existence.

This access to other planets and parts of creation enabled man to understand that there is a force holding all these elements in control: the moon, the stars, thunder, lightning and, the sun, planets. That force is the Almighty God, even though those who propagate scientific atheism tend to deny that, yet he remains the one that holds all the elements in their place.

He controls the universe by His power.

PSALM 24:1-2

"The earth is the LORD's, and the fulness thereof; the world, and they that dwell therein. For he hath founded it upon the seas, and established it upon the floods".

The other gods do not possess this ability; they only bring destruction of God's creation. Yet even in their destructive abilities, they are still limited. No god or man, with all the so-called technology of men, has been able to alter God's perfect order of arrangement of the universe. The sea, the mountains, the sky and the firmament have never moved from their positions. God Almighty is a God of order and perfect arrangement. He made day and night, and since its creation, the earth has been in the same pattern.

These other gods are gods of disorder. They operate and carry out their works in disorder, confusion, and commotion.

When man sinned against God several thousand years ago, before Christ, God separated Himself from men because they were unclean and sinful in their nature. The Almighty cannot behold sin and get close to anything that is unclean (Habakkuk 1:13).

With God's separation from man, the other gods now unleashed their evil ways on man and began to lure man into all sorts of evil and every form of wicked act, which were against God's nature, corrupting the nature of the Almighty in man without any form of redemption or cleansing for man. Even though the blood of the animal was being used in the olden days, it can't change the evil nature that corrupts man. Man began to worship them and not worship the Almighty, their true Creator, the maker of heaven and earth.

DEUTERONOMY 32:17

"They sacrificed to demons, not to God, to gods whom they have not known, new gods who came lately, whom your fathers never feared".

THE DREAM

I HAD A DREAM on the 10th day of December in the year 2023, to be precise. In that dream, I saw myself watching what was happening as if I were watching a TV programme. In the dream, I saw men making wars among themselves, mostly the Arabs.

At the time when I had that dream, there was already an ongoing war between the Israelites and Palestine. This war started on the 7th day of October of that year, and another war between Russia and Ukraine had been ongoing for a year before the second mentioned war.

In that dream, it felt like what was presently happening in the world at the time: I saw men fighting so much among themselves without giving room or a chance for reconciliation, resolution or any form of talk on peace.

While we were watching what was happening on earth at that time, men's hearts were only stirred up for war, conflict and destruction, and then suddenly, I was taken into another realm. In that realm, the place I saw did not look like earth; it looked different; the clouds and the ground of the place were not too far from each other like on earth; that is to say, while standing, one can stretch far enough to reach the clouds from the ground.

Another feature that I noticed was that the clouds had a colour that looked like a mixture of red and pink in the midst of the white clouds. Then, after I noticed all these features in that realm, I saw a personality that looked like a god but with human features. Why do I say it looks like a god? Because it had very long, majestic, flowing hair, it looked majestic and moved with so much strength and super speed, but there was something I noticed about this personality: he only did destructive acts.

This very powerful personality was fast and quick with a destructive force. It was a powerful force of destruction, and all that this personality was doing was stirring up the ocean and the sea. When it did that, I saw the water coming out of the river, ocean and sea, and the water began to come to land. It was trying to bring down the sky from its place, and it was shaking the earth. This personality was doing all sorts of destructive acts with a quick, fast and destructive force.

Then, while I saw this happening, all of a sudden, I saw another personality that looked like the first personality. In addition to its physical features, it was also very powerful and looked majestic. It could fly through the sky and move with instant speed, but the second personality was doing all he could to stop the other destructive instant force from doing its destructive acts on the planet. This second personality was also very powerful, but it moved at the same speed and strength as the destructive personality. All these two personalities looked like men, and then I woke up from the dream terrified.

When I woke from that dream, I never understood all I saw, but when the year 2024 started, I understood what I had seen in that dream, and it was both spiritual and physical—the year 2024 started with an earthquake in Japan and other places.

Also, in January 2024, in the United States of America, in states like Florida, there was a news broadcast where the water on the beach was moving towards the land and was chasing people as if it had legs. What I saw in the news was exactly how I saw it in the dream—how the destructive personality was moving the water from the ocean to the land. There were also a lot of plane crashes in the first three months of the year 2024, like something was shaking off the plane from the sky.

I do not share all of these to instigate fear in you but to point out the destructive works of these gods. As for us, all shall be well with the children of God, and amidst these trials.

CHAPTER 4

THE MANIFESTATION OF GOD AMONG MEN

One day, I woke up at 3 a.m., and immediately, I heard the still, small voice of the Holy Spirit. I always recognised that still, small voice, and it said to me, "Stand up and write."

The urgency was palpable as I reached for my pen, ready to write the message conveyed to me. These were the words I had been told to write down: The gods thought that with their deception, trickery and tactics, they could withstand the knowledge, superiority and wisdom of the Almighty God. All wisdom, knowledge and understanding belong to God the Almighty.

The gods know that God cannot behold iniquity and sin, and anything unholy, i.e., your Creator, the Almighty God, cannot get close to any form of unrighteousness because He dwelt only in holiness (Habakkuk 1:13). This means that your Creator, God, the Almighty, cannot fellowship with a corrupted nature from His nature of purity.

These other gods know this too well, and they then corrupted man's God-like nature, deceived man and separated him from God. They are so corrupted by this evil nature that man even wants to destroy anything that is of God with the help of the other gods, just like the dream I wrote about in chapter 3. In the Bible, the Almighty only walks with men who are holy and punishes those who sin. Men of old like Noah, Job and Daniel are men that God was with because they hated sin and walked in righteousness.

GENESIS 6:9

"Noah was a just man, perfect in his generation. Noah walked with God."

JOB 1:1

"There was a man in the land of Uz, whose name was Job; and that man was blameless and upright and one who feared God and shunned evil."

DANIEL 1:8

"But Daniel purposed in his heart that he would not defile himself with the portion of the king's delicacies, nor with the wine which he drank."

In biblical times, man's sins were mostly cleansed by the blood of bulls and animals and mostly by the sacrifice of blood to cleanse sin. This is so because the Almighty God created us humans from Himself; the blood that flows inside every man is the blood and the power of the Almighty God. It is actually something that is mystical and can't be explained by a mere man.

God desired to draw all humanity unto Himself, transcending the boundaries imposed by sin and corruption. Thus, He manifested Himself in the form of Yeshua, born to dwell among mortals.

1 TIMOTHY 2:5

"For there is one God and one mediator between God and mankind, the man Christ Jesus."

The purpose of Yeshua's coming was twofold: to reveal the true nature of God's love and to provide a means of redemption for humanity's sins.

When God sees a righteous man on the face of the earth, He draws close to such individual, especially men of the Bible time, men like David, Samuel, Abraham, King Asa, Jehoshaphat, etc., but these men are a fraction of His creation, mostly the Israelites. God Almighty, in His wisdom, wanted to bring all men to Himself and make us His people so that He could fellowship with man.

JOHN 12:32

"If I am lifted up from the earth, I shall draw all men to myself."

Men can serve the Almighty God and depart from those other gods that have corrupted man's nature and taken over their hearts to do evil from God's nature of purity and blamelessness. The Almighty God took another part of Himself and made it into a lamb of sacrifice. Remember, the Almighty God has the power of divine replication and divine multiplication for any form or thing He solely desires. I mentioned in the earlier Chapters that He did this by taking a part of Himself, being born into this world and becoming a man and dwelling among us. He took up the nature of a man and fellowshipped with men. He was killed and died like a man but didn't live in the corrupted ways of man.

JOHN 1:14

"And the word became flesh and dwelt among us."

The elements of darkness who now manifest themselves as gods in the heart of men knew about Yeshua [Jesus] coming into the world, but they never knew it was going to end how it did. They didn't know that God could dwell among men, be in the form of man in flesh and blood, and that flesh will not be corrupted.

1 CORINTHIANS 2:8

"Which none of the princes of this world knew; for had they known it, they would not have crucified the Lord of glory".

Let's talk about these princes of this world; one of which is the prince of death. In the past, when men wanted to get close to God, this prince of death would raise an argument over man. He would raise that man disobeyed God in the beginning when God told man not to eat of the fruit of knowledge and evil, and that if they ever eat of it, they shall surely die.

However, we serve a God who is infinite in His wisdom and His power supersedes all. He came in the form of a man, He was killed and died as a man would, and in doing this, He defeated death. He did this so that we who are made in His image and likeness, and through (Jesus), all men would be saved from the yoke of death and the destruction of their soul.

Every soul in man is important to God Almighty, the Creator, and through the name of Yeshua [Jesus], man can now have absolute and complete fellowship with the Almighty God.

Though men may die in this physical body, our souls will not die because death has been defeated by the name of Yeshua [Jesus], our Saviour, Lord and God. As humans, all we need to do is accept and believe in this free gift and victory.

ROMANS 10:9

"If you declare with your mouth, 'Jesus is Lord' and believe in your heart that God raised him from the dead, you shall be saved."

JOHN 14:19-20

"Before long, the world will not see me anymore, but you will see me. Because I live, you also will live. On that day, you would realise that I am in my father, and you are in me, and I am in you."

Praise the name of the Lord the Most High, Holy Spirit; I reference You, the Spirit of light and truth.

CHAPTER 5

GOD'S LOVE FOR MAN IN CREATION

I woke up on the 12th day of June in the year 2023 at about 5:18 a.m.; then I heard the still, small voice of the Holy Ghost say to me, "Pick up a book and write down these words." I did as I was told. I then began to write these words:

The Almighty God created humans to live without any form of worry or pain, providing them with all meat, fruits, water, and wine, like the natural palm wine from palm trees and beautiful flowers for their beauty and scent.

GENESIS 2:7-9

"And the Lord God formed man of the dust of the ground, and breathed into his nostrils the breath of life, and man became a living soul. And God planted a garden eastward in Eden, and there He put the man whom He had formed. And out of the ground made the Lord God to grow every tree that is pleasant to the sight and good for food, the tree of life also in the midst of the garden, and the tree of knowledge of good and evil."

The Almighty God made different seasons and time zones across the planet to show diversity.

GENESIS 1:14

"And the Lord said let there be light in the firmament of the heaven to divide the day from the night, and let them be for signs, and for seasons, and for days and for years."

The Almighty God made humans differently with differences in skin colour, race, culture, languages, beliefs, tribe, food, practices, and way of life, all for His pleasure and to show diversity in His creation. He created man never to suffer or want for anything.

GENESIS 1:21

"And God created great whales, and every living creature that moves, which the waters brought forth abundantly after their kind and every winged fowl after his kind, and God saw that it was good."

The Almighty God created daytime for work and play, and nighttime for rest; that is the reason why sleeping at night is always sweet and enjoyable and mostly uncontrollable. The human body was programmed for rise-up time and rest time. The Almighty God made nighttime for men to rest and not to be awake.

GENESIS 1:16-18

"And God made two great lights, the greater light to rule the day, and the lesser light to rule the night; He made the stars also, and God set them in the firmament of the heavens to give light upon the earth, and to rule over the day and over the night, and to divide the light from darkness; and God saw that it was good."

The Almighty God created all forms of pleasure for man's living, things like laughter, making jokes, socialising with one another, achieving success either in the work of their hands or from the strength of their physical body, dancing, celebrating festivities, sex in marriage, playing and taking care of the plants and animals He created, which He put under the care and authority of man.

GENESIS 2:15

"And the Lord God took the man, and put him into the Garden of Eden to dress it and to keep it."

GENESIS 1:28

"And God blessed them, and God said unto them, be fruitful and multiply, and replenish the earth, and subdue It. and have dominion over the fish of the sea and over the fowl of the air, and over every living thing that moved upon the earth."

The Almighty also created animals, herbs of the field, and birds of the air, either for man's meat, protection, or medicine.

GENESIS 1:30

"And to every beast of the earth, and to every fowl of the air, and to everything that creepeth upon the earth, wherein there is life, I have given every green herb for meat: and it was so."

The Almighty God made the waters to quench their taste, grow their crops, and clean their physical body. The water comes from the sky, the sea, and the ocean.

The Almighty God allows man to have dominion over the ocean, the sea, and the land. This is the reason why humans can swim in water, take out any quantity they can from either a river or sea or even dig out the ground to get an unstoppable quantity of water for their use.

Humans even pollute the sea and ocean; still, the water obeys them because they are God's children, having all the rights and privileges a child enjoys with his father.

The Almighty God gave man dominion over the mountains, the trees, the firmament, the clouds, the moon, galaxies, the stars and even the solar system.

That is why today, humans fly in planes like birds across the sky and the clouds; they also fly in space with space jets, and they explore other planets. They can also predict seasons and natural cosmic phenomena; this is because they have been given dominion over all the things the Almighty God made. And all that God made before man was meant to obey man.

Then the Spirit of the Lord said to me while I was still writing: the Almighty God is their King, and all humans are all Princes, having equal rights and dominion over all that was created before them.

GENESIS 1:26

"And God said, let us make in our image after our likeness, and let them have dominion over the fish of the sea, and over the fowl the air, and over the cattle, and over all the earth, and over every creeping thing that creepeth upon the earth."

The Spirit of the Lord told me to think deeply about this. While I was thinking, the Lord's Spirit said: I allow man to enjoy the pleasure of falling in love with whomever they desire in the union of marriage because I fell in love with man first. When humans fall in love, they become married in the union of marriage, which I instituted at the beginning of creation.

GENESIS 2:21-25

"And the Lord God caused a deep sleep to fall upon Adam, and he slept, and He took one of his ribs and closed up the flesh instead thereof. And the rib, which the Lord God had taken from man, made He a woman, and He brought her unto the man. And Adam said this is now bone of my bones and flesh of my flesh. She shall be called woman because she was taken out of man. Therefore shall a man leave his father and his mother and shall cleave unto his wife and they shall be one flesh, and they were both naked, the man and his wife were not ashamed."

They then engage themselves in the pleasure of sex, which is like planting a seed, which would yield a harvest, or the planting of two or three seeds of corn, which would yield about three sticks of corn. That is My nature of multiplication in creation.

That is the Almighty's intention in sexual pleasure. I put a seed in every man to produce after its kind. After a seed is planted in the act of sexual pleasure, then a child is born, which is a great joy, having to birth a child of your kind with all genetics and DNA, showing that this is yourself in a smaller form.

I gave My creation My nature of reproducing, making photocopies of themselves just as the Almighty, their Maker, made man in His smallest form to love them, care for them, and cherish them just as they do to their own children. All of creation points to how God earnestly and deeply loves man whom He made in His image.

See the beast of the land, the flow of the air and all the creeping animals on the face of the earth, which were created before the creation of man, up until this present time, they have never changed their nature. Has the lion changed from being the strongest animal? Or has the dog stopped being man's best friend? I have never seen a sheep become a cannibal because, all this time, a sheep has been a herbivorous animal. They have never changed since creation.

The Spirit of the Lord told me to think deeply about these again: Has the snake stopped crawling on his belly? Or did it begin to modernise itself from its original form and become like a goat, or did the goat start to talk like a human? Everything the Almighty God made is still in their place.

1 TIMOTHY 4:4

"For every creature of God is good, and nothing to be refused, if it be received with thanksgiving."

Everything He made knows its place in His perfect arrangement and has never gone out of its place. They all obey God. If today, the world wakes up and sees the mountain moving from where it was originally placed, how would men react? I would guess - fearful.

Then He said - "This is why I am concerned about the fate of man, my creation. They have lost their form and place and are not keen to be My children. Even though I came as their redemption, they still reject this salvation and refuse to receive this free gift of Jesus (Yeshua).

"Jesus (Yeshua) was sent as a lamb of sacrifice; the Almighty God came as a child to save man, His most loved creation. I took the form of a lamb of sacrifice, yet many continue in their evil".

ROMANS 5:17

"For if, by the trespass of the one man, death reigned through that one man, how much more will those who receive God's abundant provision of grace and of the gift of righteousness reign in life through the one man, Jesus Christ!"

That was the last word the Holy Spirit ministered to me, and I stopped writing at about 6:30 a.m.

I am led to share with all, the depth of God's love for man, which is evident in all created things. If we acknowledge that God loves us this much, then we will not yield our lives to continue under the influence of those other gods.

All glory to the Almighty God, the revealer of every deep secret, the giver of wisdom and understanding.

Amen!

CHAPTER 6

MYSTERY OF THE COMMUNION

God is the one who began to create avenues to fellowship with man and bring them into perfect communion with Himself. The other gods are incapable of this, instead, it is men that bring themselves into such communion with these gods. Those gods are not capable of beginning such a process of intimate relationship. This is why God remains no match for these ones, incomparable to any of them.

The Spirit of the Lord again ministered these words to me on the 30th day of January in the year 2024, saying:

"Do you know why Jesus Christ told His disciples to share the bread and wine as His body and blood for the cleansing of sin, and why they should do it in remembrance of Him?"

LUKE 22:19–20

"And He took bread and gave thanks, and broke it, and gave unto them, saying this is my body, which is given for you. Do this in remembrance of me. Likewise, also, the cup after supper, saying this cup is the New Testament in my blood that is shed for you."

"Yes, the body and blood of Jesus Christ is for the purification of sin," He said, and I then asked how and why.

The Spirit of the Lord ministered to me saying that man was made from God's power and likeness, and then man sinned, and his nature became corrupted. But even with man's corrupted nature, men still have the image of the Almighty God in them. Man sinned, but in redemption, when the Almighty God took a part of Himself, became man, and came as a lamb of sacrifices, [Yeshua] Jesus gave up His physical body and blood for our redemption from that very sin and the corruption that separates man from the Almighty God the Creator.

Then Jesus instructed His disciples to take bread and break among themselves, likewise, the wine, which became the New Testament, meaning the new law and order for man's living. This is actually a physical sacrifice of Himself for our redemption from corruption. This implies that, as Christians and believers in this free gift of salvation, we should endeavour to always take the physical bread and physical wine for the cleansing and purification of our mortal body while we are in this present body. By praying on it, it turns into His blood and body through the power of the Holy Ghost.

HEBREWS 9:22

"In fact, the law requires that nearly everything be cleansed with blood, and without the shedding of blood, there is no forgiveness."

As believers in this salvation who live in this present world, we must continue to engage in this spiritual practice so as to purify our mortal body from the yoke that sin brings into it. Yokes like sickness and diseases were brought through sin. Also, the regular intake of Holy Communion by believers would restore in our physical body all that man has lost in sin—wealth, health, boldness, fruitfulness, strength, peace, etc.

EPHESIANS 1:7

"In Him, we have redemption through His blood, the forgiveness of sin, in accordance with the riches of God's grace."

And with the communion, we can withstand and overcome the wicked acts of evil and darkness that possess our physical body. For believers to remain strong, healthy, fruitful and productive with a sound mind in this present life that we live in, the communion table with brethren and family is a must-meal.

LEVITICUS 17:11

"For the life of a creature is in the blood, and I have given it to you to make atonement for yourself on the altar; it is the blood that makes atonement for one's life."

REVELATION 1:5

"And from Jesus Christ, who is the faithful witness, the firstborn from the dead, and the ruler of the kings of the earth. To Him who loves us and has freed us from our sins by His blood."

Communion brings man redemption from corruption of the body. Considering that it is a clear command from Jesus, the sharing of unleavened bread and drinking of wine among the brethren of faith is a must, as it is a daily meal for our physical body to perform optimally.

Just as when a doctor prescribes multivitamins for proper body function to improve the immune system and replenish lost natural vitamins in the body, that is how the Holy Communion acts as the believers' vitamin against the evil and destruction that sin brought to both our physical and our spiritual body. Just as I explained in Chapter 1, man was made in the likeness and nature of God, and according to Genesis 1:27, God in His nature cannot be sick, feeble, hungry, weak, poor, wicked, unfruitful, depressed, mentally unstable, etc. All these things make man unhappy on earth. The Almighty God did not make man with all these attributes, but because of sin, man's godly nature became weak.

God made Himself into a man as Yeshua, Jesus, the lamb of sacrifice, a higher self than the natural man, and died for our sins so we could be saved through His blood. We believers who live in this world will have redemption through His sacrifices. The blood and body of Jesus, in the communion of unleavened bread and wine, would, by the power of the Holy Ghost, quicken our mortal body and then replenish our physical body and our soul.

1 JOHN 1:7

"But if we walk in the light, as He is in the light, we have fellowship with one another, and the blood of Jesus, His Son, purifies us from all sin."

1 PETER 1:18–19

"For you know that it was not with perishable things such as silver or gold that you were redeemed from the empty ways of life handed down to you from your ancestors, but with the precious blood of Christ, a lamb without blemish or defect."

The communion is a must-have spiritual meal for all who believe in the free gift of salvation to live their God-ordained lives and destiny in this present life.

God has made provisions for us to enjoy life, we must keep this in mind as we daily live with the intention of living as those who have overcome the gods of this world.

CHAPTER 7

GOD'S MYSTERIOUS WORK ON THE HUMAN SOUL

I woke up in the early hours of the morning to pray, and after my devotion, I sat meditating, and the still, small voice of the Holy Spirit began to speak to me again. I took up my book and wrote. These are the words:

"The only thing that man needs to worry about after this present life is his soul".

MATTHEW 10:28

"And do not fear those who kill the body but cannot kill the soul. Rather fear Him who can destroy both soul and body in hell."

MATTHEW 16:26

"For what would it profit a man if he gains the whole world and lost his soul? Or what shall a man give in return for his soul?"

Men should strive to keep their souls purified and stainless from any form of sin or defilement.

1 THESSALONIANS 5:23

"Now may the Lord of peace Himself sanctify you completely, and may your whole Spirit and soul and body be kept blameless at the coming of our Lord Jesus Christ."

It is absolutely impossible for man to achieve such a feat in their daily living because of the corrupted nature that inhabits man. But by God's love and mercies, man was given a second chance, that when this physical body is dead, man's soul will be revived. This can only happen by the name of Jesus; the name of Jesus is the only purification for man's soul, and the blood of Jesus is the blood that cleanses the soul of man, and makes it possible for the soul to be revived after death.

1 CORINTHIANS 15:35-39

"But someone will ask, "How are the dead raised? With what kind of body will they come?" How foolish! What you sow does not come to life unless it dies. When you sow, you do not plant the body that will be, but just a seed, perhaps of wheat or of something else. But God gives it a body as he has determined, and to each kind of seed, he gives its own body. Not all flesh is the same: People have one kind of flesh, animals have another, birds another and fish another."

1 CORINTHIANS 6:19-20

"Or do you not know that your body is a temple of the Holy Spirit within you, whom you have from God? You are not your own, for you were bought with a price. So glorify God in your body."

Every man living today lives and survives by the blood; without the blood that flows through our veins, no man can live; the blood holds the life and death of man. When man sinned in the beginning, man's blood became corrupted from the nature of God and the light of God that inhabits our body, soul, and blood.

LEVITICUS 17:11

"For the life of the flesh is in the blood; and I have given it to you upon the altar to make an atonement for your soul; for it's the blood that makes atonement for the soul."

But God, in His love for man, took a part of Himself as Jesus, our Saviour, who died and lives again. The blood of Jesus is then inoculated into our blood to sanctify us and purify man from the corrupted blood that man carries through sin, but the blameless and the stainless blood of Jesus purified the contaminated blood of man so as to bring man purified and sanctified blood through the sacrifice of Jesus Christ, which saves us all.

If any man does not receive this free gift of Jesus Christ for the sanctification of their soul, then such soul would be destroyed, i.e., it shall not be revived after death; it shall be destroyed in hell because anything unclean cannot see God or be part of the Almighty God.

God's intention in creating man was for man to believe in Him, have fellowship with Him, worship Him, and all humans to love each other and care for or tend to the things the Almighty God created. Then everything changed when the first man sinned; then man became unclean before God, and men began to practice all sorts of religions, doctrines, and beliefs, saying that they were worshiping God the Almighty.

But in actual fact, behind the scenes, they are in the worship of the other gods, which are gods of men, because from creation, the only doctrine that God handed to man was to take care of all that He has created. That man should fellowship with Him describes His love for man because what you love, you care for. This is the same love and care God showed to man in creation and after creation, before the fall of man.

Certainly, with sin, God rejected man not because He hates us but because of the corruption that is in us, and He can't behold sin.

HABAKKUK 1:13

"Your eyes are too pure to look on evil; you cannot tolerate wrongdoing. Why, then, do you tolerate the treacherous? Why are you silent while the wicked swallow up those more righteous than themselves?"

We can see His purity in creation with everything that was made and created, whether through the plants, trees, waters, seas, oceans, atmosphere, firmaments, rain, sun, moon, stars, galaxy, sand, mountains, stones, the air we breathe, pure, clean oxygen, the snow, etc. They are all clean and pure in their original state of creation. They are God's wonder in creation and are natural and pure always, if not polluted by man's evil activities.

GENESIS 1:31

"And God saw everything that He had made, and behold, it was very good. And the evening and the morning were the sixth day."

All glory and praise be unto the name of Yeshua, Jesus Christ, the one who saves our souls from destruction. Amen.

CHAPTER 8

THE BATTLE AGAINST THE CHILDREN OF THE ALMIGHTY GOD

Man's godly nature has been corrupted for thousands of years since the gods have contaminated human hearts. However, in His boundless mercy, God sent Yeshua, Jesus Christ, two thousand years ago for man's redemption. The Messiah came in human form, taking on human nature but also possessing the characteristics of the Almighty God to complete His mission of rescuing mankind from the sin that destroys man's soul and the gods that corrupt man's soul.

Then, after Yeshua left the world, He descended into hell, took the key of life for the redemption of man, and ascended into heaven. This is the good news of His free gift of redemption and soul-saving mission for man, which is now being preached across the world. His disciples were the first to send His redemptive message of a second chance of man's salvation. First to His people, the Jews, then later to the Gentiles, meaning all nations. Then, that very good news of redemption has been moving from the 1st century till this very present time in the 21st century. The free gift of Jesus is preached to all nations across the world, and above, even underneath the earth, Jesus is being preached.

There is something so fascinating about this: the Almighty God even uses the one who crucified Jesus to spread the Gospel, like the Romans, the Greeks, etc. They were the ones that forced other nations to accept Jesus when they colonised these nations. But behind the scenes, they were actually subtly worshipping their pagan gods. But the name of Jesus overshadows their ways and pagan worship.

Man began to accept the gift of (Yeshua) Jesus as the Saviour of man from sins that had held him down in captivity, and for man to fellowship with God again as his Maker, he began to gradually turn away from the worship of the other gods, i.e., idolatry. Still, there are many who do not understand the message of this free gift and salvation being preached to them. Humans still worship idols and pagan gods. However, the name of Jesus is taking over every corner of the earth and across the nations of the world with the radical biblical messages written by the disciples of Jesus, through the inspiration of the Holy Spirit.

We can see this outpouring of the Holy Spirit by the breaking out of the evangelical Pentecostal Gospel missions preaching and teaching only from the Holy Bible, which is the true word of God and not the doctrines of men. With the outpouring of the Holy Spirit, man began to walk in the path of God the Almighty, the Creator and the Everlasting King. Man began to drop and abandon the worship of the pagan idol (gods). These are the gods that pollute the hearts of men.

When men sinned against God, they began to purge themselves with the blood of Jesus for their redemption. Man also began to thrive for holy living with the help of the Holy Spirit, the Comforter.

But something happened; the other gods noticed that man were gradually growing in the worship of God and no longer worship them or offer sacrifices to them, (in some cultures and religions, they even offer up their children and generations, even yet unborn, to these gods for rituals and worship), they began to scheme harder against man and attack the sons of God with all sort of evil and darkness that the world has never seen before.

I will give a practical example of all that I have been trying to say in this chapter.

THE DREAM

IN THE YEAR 2020, on the 3rd day in January, to be precise, I had a dream. In that dream, I saw people sick; humans were very sick. I saw people in the hospital, some on the floor, and others in the hospital bathrooms, others on the bed, and there was no place to accommodate them. They were just hanging around the hospital. There were so many sick people at the same time. Then I turned from that very view, and I saw a doctor looking frustrated; he was trying all he could to make the people better and save their lives, but it seemed nothing was working; it was to no avail. Then I noticed another significant thing that was happening: the doctor I saw trying to treat the people who were sick was an Asian, and he was also putting a covering over the patients' head region to make them feel better. But again, to no avail.

Another notable thing I noticed in this dream was that the patients I saw in that hospital were mostly white-skinned, and a few black-skinned people were sick among them. Then, in that very dream again, I asked in my spirit, "How can we be saved from this sickness that seems to be consuming men in this manner?"

I heard a word being spoken to me, saying, "And you should say this word daily. HOLY GHOST FIRE, LET THE FIRE OF THE HOLY GHOST FOLLOW ME/US." Then, I woke up from the dream, terrified.

I told my husband about it, and I told him that a disease was coming and was going to be devastating around the whole world, and that was when we started praying in this manner: the fire of the Holy Ghost, let the fire of the Holy Ghost follow me. I sent the same message to all my loved ones and some friends and neighbours about my dream and how they needed to pray for the year. Thanks and glory be to the name of Jesus that none of our family or friends was consumed during that pandemic.

But actually, before I saw this very dream, there was a report of a flu disease outbreak in China called Noval Coronavirus, which was making people sick, and people were visiting hospitals, that was in December 2019. But it wasn't a thing of concern to the whole world, not until January through February 2020. In March, the World Health Organisation (WHO) declared a global pandemic, and countries across the globe were shut down for fear of contamination. Even now, when COVID-19 is no longer a major threat to human existence, scientists have not been able to discover what was the initial cause or origin of the virus that killed humans in millions within that very short time.

But here is the answer: every evil in life is orchestrated by the enemy leveraging the capacity of human beings. The gods of this world who orchestrate destruction will always seize sicknesses, natural disasters and even human disasters to achieve their aim of destroying life and creations of God.

After the pandemic rescinded, and all the destruction and disruption that it brought to man, (livelihood, human lives, human freedom, families, mental health, marriages, etc.) then a vaccine was discovered to destroy the virus or reduce its potency of killing humans, and with the vaccine, humans began to be free again. This was mostly through the prayers of the saints of Yeshua. Donald Trump, the American President at the time of the pandemic, made a remarkable statement in a press conference when he said that if the hospitals are kept open, why then shut the doors of the churches? The church is a place where people go for prayers and healing. This is one of the questions that can tell you that the enemy is leveraging such a situation to achieve his aim of attacking the children of God.

Then, in the year 2021, after the pandemic had subsided, my country experienced serious security challenges; people were being kidnapped and killed aimlessly on a daily basis, and it seemed there was little or nothing the government and security agents could do to stop or reduce the situation, It was really terrifying.

My family and I packed our bags, and we left for the United Kingdom for studies. That very year, we just wanted to stay out of our country for the time being until the security issues got better. On the other hand, I was so happy to study again. When we got to the United Kingdom, everyone was mandated to take the COVID-19 vaccine. I was not okay with it, but I had to take it anyway because without taking the vaccine in the UK, you would experience a lot of restrictions. I took the first shot of the vaccine in November 2021; that very night of the day I took the vaccine, I had a dream, and in that dream, I saw an entity - she was huge, had long, flowing hair, and had a human image. Still, she did not behave like a human; I saw her using her feet to trample upon humans, I saw her standing close to the seashore, and saying many things with a loud voice, many of which I would not want to share here.

However, after that night, it became very clear to me that the situation was one orchestrated by the princes of this world to destroy the lives, faith and works of men. The entire season was targeted at shutting down the teaching of salvation and repentance from sin to all tribes, tongues and nations. Hence, men were given new issues to focus on while churches were locked.

In that dream, I was shouting and praying in a loud voice, too that the church of God cannot be destroyed, then I woke up from the dream, terrified.

CHAPTER 9

MARRIAGE AS A MANIFESTATION OF THE ALMIGHTY GOD

One of the manifestations of God that sets Him apart from other gods is the institution of marriage, which no one else can lay claim to its foundation, except God. God Himself ordained the union of marriage. Before the fall of man in the Garden of Eden, the Almighty God instituted the union of marriage. According to the Bible, when God created the earth, He created all the fowl of the air and the beasts of the field; they were all in two pairs, male and female, and for man, a woman was created.

Initially, man, who was made in God's image and likeness, was all alone, but the Almighty God, in all His wisdom and knowledge, immediately noticed that there was a defect in man, and then He made him a support, which is the woman.

GENESIS 2:20

"And Adam gave names to all cattle's, and to the fowl of the air, and to every beast of the field; but for Adam, there was not found a help meet for him."

GENESIS 2:21

"So the Lord God caused the man to fall into a deep sleep; and while he was sleeping, he took one of the man's ribs and closed up the place with flesh."

The Almighty God saw that the man was lonely. He then made the woman from the man's body; this is to show God's power of multiplication and duplication in creation.

GENESIS 2:22

"And the rib, which the Lord God had taken from man, made He a woman, and brought her unto the man."

The rib bone that God took from man is very significant in the union of marriage. It actually means support and protection. In human anatomy, the rib cage bone protects and supports very important organs in the body, like the heart, which is the light of God in man, and other parts, like the lungs.

The rib cage supports the proper function of the lungs, allowing for breathing. With this very little scientific analogy, we can then deduce that the woman was formed from the man for his own support, protection and life. She is a part of his entire life. It can then be said that the union of marriage was instituted for the protection and support of the man to achieve his purpose on earth, and a man must find his rib cage bone to support, protect and enable him to live his own destiny.

GENESIS 2:23

"And Adam said this is now the bone of my bones and flesh of my flesh; she shall be called woman because she was taken out of man."

From human statistical evidence in the study and research of the behaviour of men, and even from medical science research, we can see that men who are not married or have female companions may not function well in their daily lives; some men can hardly cope without a woman. Some do, but a few do not because if a man desires the companionship of a woman and he is not getting it, he may feel lost and, most of the time, empty, as does a woman. This is intertwined, and this is why almost every human from ancient times to the present desires or partakes in the institution of marriage according to different cultures, tribes and religions. Only God could be so mindful of man's need in this way to provide a companion for him.

Just as the rib cage bone supports, protects and allows for breathing, so too is the union of marriage. The union of marriage protects both the man and the woman in matrimony from any issues that come their way. Trust is everything in any relationship, and so too is it in the union of marriage. The union of marriage brings support to the woman and the man. They are to help each other in support and protection, bringing balance in the function of daily human living to fulfil their God-given purpose on earth, and they are to support each other to raise children in a proper functional way. The union of marriages also enables the man and the woman to actually breathe; it makes them feel alive.

If you are married and you have sex with your partner, you will agree with me that when a couple shares their body as a gift to one another and experiences an orgasm, they feel alive and, most of the time, completely transcended. This is the feeling that comes with being married. In that instance, it also promotes mental stability, joy, and happiness. This is the gift the Almighty God blessed mankind with.

GENESIS 2:24

"Therefore shall a man leave his father and his mother, and shall cleave unto his wife, and they shall be one flesh."

The Almighty God instituted the union of marriage for peace, companionship, life, protection, support, oneness, friendship, and most importantly, worship and fellowship with the Almighty, our Maker and for humans to take care of what God has created and for man to be fruitful and multiply. But when man sinned, he gave room for these other gods to usurp the real intent of the union of marriage which God instituted Himself.

One of the first creations that the other gods attacked was the union of marriage, by first breaking their trust in God and then between the man and the woman. When man told God in the garden that 'it was the woman that you gave me …,' when they had sinned, that implies that their protective barrier was already broken by the fall, which affects marriages today. We now see a lack of trust, love, support, protection or balance in marriages.

GENESIS 3:9, 12 & 25

"And the Lord God called unto Adam, and said unto him, Where art thou?"

"And the man said, The woman whom thou gavest to be with me, she gave me of the tree, and I did eat."

"And they were both naked, the man and his wife, and were not ashamed."

It was never recorded in the Bible that the first man and woman, Adam and Eve, must have hated themselves after living together for a long time, but from the story of Cain and Abel we can assume that Cain learnt strife and envy from somewhere, perhaps such was already in their midst. From Cain's story, we can see envy, jealousy, and destruction, as well as he killed his brother, which are the kind of destructive works that these other gods engineer.

GENESIS 4:8

"And Cain said to Abel, his brother, 'Let us go out to the field.' And when they were in the field, Cain rose against Abel, his brother and slew him."

That is why the union of marriage has been under attack from the very beginning of its creation until this present time from the other gods operating in the heart and space of man, destroying marriages and families. Even the relationship between the couple can be destroyed, their children will be easily reached by the enemy.

We can see this today in the different names given to the union of marriages, which was not the real marriage institution ordained by the Almighty God. Different names like polygamy, the marriage between a man and many women or polyandry, the marriage of a woman to different men. Also, gay marriage, the union of a man and a man or lesbianism, marriage between a woman and a woman. Some other tribes and religions even practice incest, the marriage between people of the same family.

In medical science, this very act causes health risks and genetic disorders Some humans are even married to animals. These are all the works of the gods; the Almighty God did not ordain this. We can see this in His word in the passage below:

GENESIS 2:24

"Therefore shall a man leave his father and his mother, and said cleave unto his wife and they shall be one flesh."

The word of God promotes marriage as a union between a man and a woman, not a man and two or more women, or a woman and two men or more; neither does it say a man and a man or a woman and a woman, or a man with his sister or a woman with her cat or dog.

The other gods corrupted the heart of man from ancient times, always making a counterfeit of every good thing that the Almighty God made. This counterfeit in marriage breeds all the chaos we see in marriages today: lack of trust, hate, immorality, and a lack of love and care. Couples deceive one another even when they live together and sleep on the same bed. This is not God's intention for the union of marriage, and these attributes are not God's nature.

God is love; how can one be in the union of marriage without love for the one you are married to? You see a man engaging in sexual pleasure with a strange woman outside the union, and so too is the wife; both are committing an abomination. The Almighty God can never be in such a home or marriage. The only thing that would inhabit such a union would eventually be darkness, and such a union would produce evil. That is what is happening to humans today.

Most of the problem the world faces today comes from the family through the union of marriages, or the birth of offspring either through marriages or outside marriages, with what we see today most of the union between a woman and a man either in marriages or outside of marriages contributes one way or another in the raising of a generation that fears God or the one that follows other gods.

Let us all be wise in the Holy Spirit and accept Jesus into our marriages and families that we may teach our children and, in turn, generations ahead would purge themselves. Let us make sure that our marriages and homes are covered in the blood of Jesus and stand purified from every form of defilement and sin that destroy marriages and families.

AMEN!

CHAPTER 10

ALMIGHTY GOD AS THE HOPE OF MAN

The reason the gods are able to lure many men into worship of themselves and deviation from God, is because they sell the idea of self-sufficiency to man. Man, in the pursuit of making himself perfect begins to fall into the snares of the enemy as they pursue those things that they think will make their lives perfect. It was Eve's pursuit of perfection and becoming like God that made her fall into the trap of the enemy.

Man, in his nature, can never be perfect or righteous. No matter the spiritual or physical work of a man to get cleansed from sin, it is the blood of Jesus that can make a man perfect and clean from the sin that corrupted his nature from the beginning.

Many men perform some good works in church and in society. Yes, these good works are good, but they can't make any perfect nor cleanse them from their sins, hence they can't make them righteous.

These acts of goodness and charity can only make the soul of a man feel good, but can't set him free. Not even the spiritual works of mercy can make a man holy; only the blood of Jesus, the Saviour and Redeemer of our soul, can save man.

The only hope that man was given for a second chance at life is the blood of Jesus, not through works but by faith and believing that the blood of Christ saved us from our sin, as well as the acceptance of this free gift of salvation.

Just like when a woman is told by the doctor that she is pregnant and that she will soon have a baby, remember that she did not see a physical baby with her naked eyes; it was only confirmed through a blood test. But through her faith in that blood test, she believed the words of the doctor or the physician who confirmed her pregnancy. She accepted this good news and began to prepare herself, both physically and mentally, for the arrival of the baby. Later, in nine months, the blood that was not seen physically becomes a baby, which she can then carry physically. This is how we must accept the gift of Yeshua, Jesus, as our Lord and Saviour, not by works but by faith.

The only work we do in this process is the work of acceptance and believing totally in this gift for the cleansing of our sin and a second chance at life.

EPHESIANS 2:8–9

"For by grace are ye saved through faith, and that not of yourself it is the gift of God, not of works, lest any man should boast."

ROMANS 10:3

"For they being ignorant of God's righteousness and going about to establish their own righteousness, have not submitted themselves unto the righteousness of God."

Human nature can't change easily from its corrupted nature even after salvation; it is only when an individual accepts Jesus Christ in their life as their Saviour and thrives daily to live holy through their spiritual commitment to the things of God, which are great and having fellowship with the God, that such a person can be free from the influence of the corrupted nature.

It is actually impossible for men to be righteous on their own. It is only through the blood of Jesus that a man can be righteous. It is the help of the Holy Spirit that enables man to make the right choices for daily living. All glory to God and to His Holy name for sending Jesus for our salvation and true righteousness.

ROMANS 3:10

"As it is written, there is none righteous, no not one."

ISAIAH 64:6

"But we are all as an unclean thing, and all our righteousness are as filthy rags; and we all do fade as and our iniquities, like the wind, have taken us away."

LUKE 18:9

"And He also told this parable to some people who trusted in themselves that they were righteous and viewed others with contempt."

ANOTHER STRANGE DREAM

IN THE YEAR 2022, on the 23rd day of February, I had another dream. In my dream, I saw a war-like scenario; it looked really dark and scary, and I saw white people dying in their thousands.

What was killing these people looked like a small black bird, but I noticed something: the bird, as small as it was, was very strong and powerful, and it destroyed men instantly without giving one a chance to escape its wrath and torture. Nothing could stop the bird's destruction. I noticed another thing: I was scared, and there were some other people around me, but I heard a voice say to me that we would be spared, and then I woke up terrified. Again, the very day I woke up from that dream, the war between Ukraine and Russia started until the present day.

I was told in that dream that nothing could stop the force of the destruction of that small bird. So, when I saw the war in Ukraine and Russia, I feared that if it was a direct manifestation of this dream, then it would most likely not stop as soon as everyone thinks.

What is happening in the world today is a clear sign from the Almighty God to humans, and it is a call to repentance. God is still giving humans a second chance to change from their evil ways. There are so many fearful things happening, but still, humans are even more evil, corrupted and wicked. Hate, lust, pride, ungratefulness, disobedience to parents, immorality, and all sorts of evil take their seats in the heart and space of man, just like the time of Noah.

Just like the time when the Israelites were in the land of Egypt, the Almighty God sent all the plaques of destruction to the Egyptians so that Pharaoh could have a change of heart so that the Israelites could go, but no, it was until the destruction came and it was already too late, that was when Pharaoh changed his heart.

Let us reflect on our lives daily to check if there is any filthiness in us. Let us allow the blood of Jesus to wash us clean, and then the Highest God will have mercy on us and on our souls. God Almighty would then place His blood of exemption upon us.

The subsequent connection to the Ukraine-Russia conflict serves as a reminder that real-world events often reflect deeper spiritual truths. Just as the dream depicted an urgent call for repentance, real-life calamities remind us of the need to confront our own self-righteousness. It urges us to recognise that true righteousness comes not from our deeds but from genuine humility and repentance.

Drawing parallels to biblical plagues, the dream suggests that, like Pharaoh, individuals often resist change until faced with overwhelming evidence of their need to repent. This resistance is a hallmark of self-righteousness, which blinds individuals to their own flaws and the need for divine intervention.

In this context, the call to examine one's heart and seek cleansing through Jesus is a powerful counter to self-righteousness. It underscores the importance of humility, self-awareness, and the acknowledgement of our dependence on God's grace rather than our own perceived merits. Ultimately, this dream serves as a profound reminder of the dangers of self-righteousness and the urgent need for true repentance and humility in seeking God's protection and mercy.

CONCLUSION

In conclusion, this book is profound and thought-provoking. It explores some of the biggest questions and mysteries of human existence. Through the guidance of the Holy Spirit; the book offers insights into the person of God, His creatures and that which lures them away from Him.

The emphasis on the importance of righteousness and a deeper understanding of our connection to God is particularly noteworthy.

We have witnessed the incredible potential of human creativity, made in the image of our Creator. We have beheld the unfathomable love of Jesus, who came as Yeshua to bridge the gap between heaven and earth. We have explored the mysteries of communion, the human soul and the fierce battle waged against the children of God. Through it all, we have seen the thread of God's righteousness, which is not our own self-righteousness but a gift of His grace.

May the understanding received from this book, ignite a fire of passion and purpose within us so that we may live as children of the Almighty, reflecting His love and glory to a world in need. May we forever cherish the truth that we are not just mere mortals but beloved sons and daughters of the Most High God, created to reign with Him in glory.

www.ingramcontent.com/pod-product-compliance
Lightning Source LLC
LaVergne TN
LVHW041251150826
845673LV00008B/2545

* 9 7 8 9 7 8 6 0 9 8 2 2 7 *